LIFESKILLS IN ACTION

JOB SKILLS

Employee Rights

M.G.
HIGGINS

W9-BON-139

LIFESKILLS IN ACTION
JOB SKILLS

MONEY

Living on a Budget | Road Trip
Opening a Bank Account | The Guitar
Managing Credit | High Cost
Using Coupons | Get the Deal
Planning to Save | Something Big

LIVING

Smart Grocery Shopping | Shop Smart
Doing Household Chores | Keep It Clean
Finding a Place to Live | A Place of Our Own
Moving In | Pack Up
Cooking Your Own Meals | Dinner Is Served

JOB

Preparing a Resume | Not Her Job
Finding a Job | Dream Jobs
Job Interview Basics | Job Ready
How to Act Right on the Job | Choices
Employee Rights | Not So Sweet

SADDLEBACK
EDUCATIONAL PUBLISHING
www.sdlback.com

ISBN-13: 978-1-68021-412-3
ISBN-10: 1-68021-412-8
eBook: 978-1-63078-813-1

Printed in Malaysia

21 20 19 18 17   1 2 3 4 5

Workers in the US have **rights**.

There are rules.

Some rules are laws.

Companies must obey them.

People must be treated fairly.

Laws keep people safe.

They help workers.

Companies are helped too.

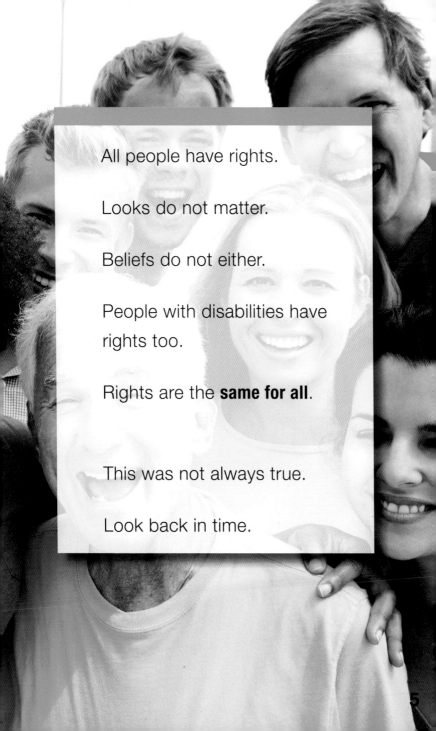

All people have rights.

Looks do not matter.

Beliefs do not either.

People with disabilities have
rights too.

Rights are the **same for all**.

This was not always true.

Look back in time.

Many children worked.

They did not go to school.

Some had hard jobs.

Jobs were **not safe**.

Workers got hurt.

Others died.

People got hurt in meat plants.

Body parts got cut off.

Mines fell in.

Workers got trapped.

They ran out of air.

Rocks crushed others.

People were not paid well.

Many worked hard.

Yet they got little money.

They had earned more.

But the company kept it.

Things were not fair.

Workers got mad.

People talked.

They joined **unions**.

Leaders spoke up.

The people in charge heard them.

Laws were passed.

Changes were made.

Things got better.

This was in the 1900s.

9

Workers have more rights now.

Some are US laws.

Others are state laws.

Look online.

Find out your rights.

Minimum wage is one right.

This is pay for an hour of work.

The US has a law.

All workers must be paid a set amount.

They can get more.

But they cannot get less.

Overtime is a right.

People may work long hours.

They make more money.

This can be 1.5 times their pay.

It may be double.

Jobs pay more on some days.

A person may work on a holiday.

Pay might be time and a half.

Some places pay double.

Being safe at work is a right.

There are laws about this.

Machines must work well.

Workers have to wear **safety gear**.

This can be gloves, hats, or boots.

Fire safety tools have to be there.

First aid kits must be too.

Exits need clear signs.

Bathrooms must be clean.

Companies cannot show **bias**.

They cannot treat one group better.

All people must be treated the same.

Facts about Bias

Can be based on:

- race
- gender
- disability
- religion
- age

Can affect:

- hiring
- pay
- job performance
- promotions
- firing

Bias can happen in many ways.

Here are **three examples**.

A worker tells a joke.

It is about a group of people.

A company posts a job.

Two people want it.

One is a man.

The other is a woman.

Both apply for the job.

They come in for interviews.

Everyone likes them.

They worry about the woman.

She might have a baby.

Then she would need time off.

They choose the man.

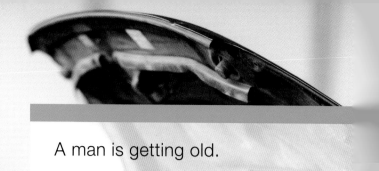

A man is getting old.

His boss wants someone younger.

The company can pay a young person less.

The man gets **fired**.

A young man gets his job.

All of these are bias.

This is not okay.

The law says so.

Laws help people with disabilities.

A worker might get a special chair.

She may need more training.

Harassment is against the law.

It is not okay.

Companies can help.

Check the handbook at work.

Follow the steps.

Examples of harassment:

- Pushing someone to go on a date

- Making comments about a person's body

- Picking on someone

- Bullying

23

People have a right to breaks.

They get time to eat too.

This is personal time.

Workers can rest.

It is not for work.

Workers have a right to **privacy**.

This does not apply to all things.

People may need to take drug tests.

Bosses can read emails.

They can hear phone calls too.

This is only for work calls.

It is not for personal calls.

Many companies offer **benefits**.

These are not rights.

Companies choose what to do.

Savings plans are a benefit.

Health insurance is another.

What if a person loses a job?

They still have rights.

There are **unemployment benefits**.

People get a part of their pay.

It helps people pay for things.

But there are rules.

The person must look for a job.

Not all workers get this.

People who quit or get fired may not.

Each state has its own rules.

UNEMPLOYMENT
OFFICE

→

Please Wait
in Line

Workers have rights.

Some are for all people.

Others are for certain states.

Which affect you?

Read the handbook at work.

It lists the rights.

Benefits are listed too.

Look online for laws.

Jobs should be pleasant.

Workers must be safe.

All people must be treated fairly.

There are laws.

Companies must obey them.

Know your rights.

What happens when a boss teases his workers and calls them names? Find out in *Not So Sweet*. Want to read on?

JUST *flip* THE BOOK!

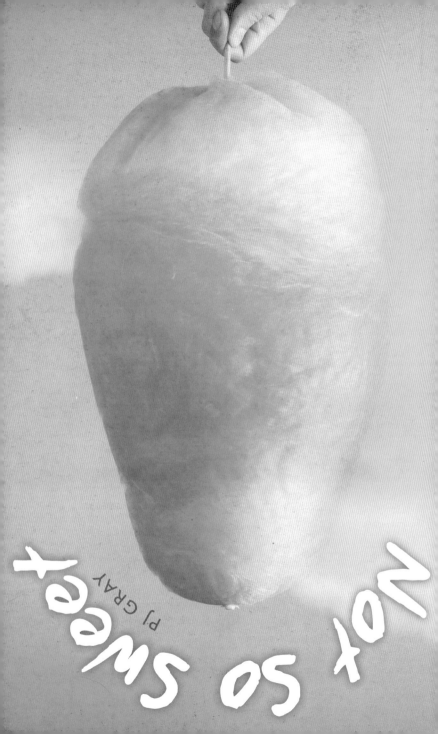

LIFESKILLS IN ACTION
JOB SKILLS

SADDLEBACK
EDUCATIONAL PUBLISHING
www.sdlback.com

All source images from Shutterstock.com

ISBN-13: 978-1-68021-412-3
ISBN-10: 1-68021-412-8
eBook: 978-1-63078-813-1

Printed in Malaysia

21 20 19 18 17   1 2 3 4 5

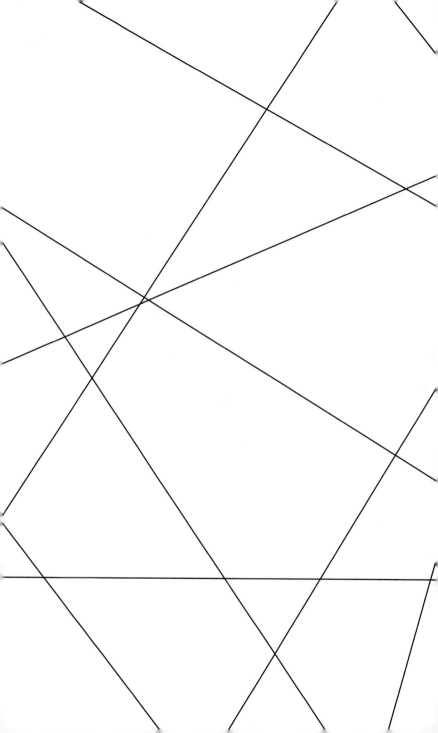

Kenny worked at So Sweet. It was a chain of candy stores. His store was in Maine. The home office was in Boston.

So Sweet was a special store. They sold all kinds of candy. There were handmade treats too. They were known for their ice cream. People loved their cotton candy. You could even buy local taffy.

Kenny had just been promoted. He had started as a cashier. The store he worked at was in Vermont. Now he was a manager. This was his first big job. He had moved to Maine for it.

There were three people on his team. One was Joan. She had worked at So Sweet for many years. She handled the handmade treats.

Beth and Monica had been there a few months. Both went to a nearby college. The girls helped customers. They could work the cash register too.

It was a good team. Joan was excellent at her job. She knew all the ice cream flavors by heart. People loved her. She had a warm, kind way.

Beth was great at the cash register. No one was faster. She was a natural.

Monica was the best at helping customers. There were rows and rows of candy. But Monica knew them all. She knew just where each candy was.

Kenny was happy to have such great workers. He was proud of his team.

One day Joan was in the stock room. She was getting some blueberry ice cream. A man stepped up to the counter.

"Granny!" Kenny called. "You have a customer."

Joan stepped from the stock room. *Was Kenny talking to her?*

"What can I get you?"

The man got some cotton candy. He left with a smile.

Joan hurried back to the stock room. Kenny had embarrassed her. Joan was older. But she was not yet a grandmother. She knew her gray hair made her look like one. But Kenny should not have said that.

Maybe it was just this one time. She would try to forget about it.

Kenny did it again the next day. Joan was upset.

"Please don't call me that."

"I'm just having fun with you, Granny," Kenny said.

"Kenny, please stop."

"Where is your sense of humor?"

Joan walked back to the stock room.
She did not like Kenny's teasing.

Beth called in sick later that week. She had a bad cold. Kenny told her to rest up and get better.

"We're down a honey today," Kenny said. He was talking to Joan and Monica.

"What?" Joan asked.

"Beth is out sick."

"But what did you call her? A honey?"

"Oh Joan, I'm just teasing," Kenny said.

Monica giggled. Joan frowned.

Later, Monica and Joan were alone. "That didn't bother you? What Kenny said?" Joan asked.

"The honey thing? He's our boss. What are you going to do?"

Beth was back at work a few days later.
She was feeling much better.

"I've got my honeys back," Kenny said.

"What?" Beth asked.

"He calls us his honeys," Monica said.

"Not cool," Beth said. "Kenny, please don't do that."

"Why do you have to be so serious? I'm just having fun."

A few days later, a woman with a suit came in. "Where can I find Kenny?"

Kenny stepped out of the stock room. "I'm right here."

The woman stuck out her hand. "I'm Mrs. Wheeler. I'm from the home office in Boston."

"Very nice to meet you," Kenny said.

"Where can we talk alone?" Mrs. Wheeler asked.

The two stepped into the stock room. Kenny closed the door behind them.

The door opened a few minutes later. Kenny looked upset. He looked around the store. There were no customers.

"Beth and Joan, will you come here please?"

They stepped into the room. "This is Mrs. Wheeler," Kenny said. "She works for So Sweet at the home office. Mrs. Wheeler is in human resources."

"Hello," Mrs. Wheeler said. "I've spoken with both of you on the phone. Thank you for calling with your concerns. I believe Kenny has something to say."

"I owe you both an apology," Kenny said. "Joan, I called you Granny. Beth, I called you honey. You both asked me to stop. And I didn't. I should have treated you better. You deserve respect."

Both Joan and Beth nodded.

Kenny kept going. "I am very sorry. It won't happen again."

"Thank you," Joan said.

"I appreciate that," Beth said.

"Thank you," Mrs. Wheeler said. "Beth, will you ask Monica to come see me?"

Kenny, Beth, and Joan stepped out of the stock room. Monica came in.

"Will you please close the door?" Mrs. Wheeler introduced herself. She explained why she was there.

"What does this have to do with me?" Monica asked.

"I wanted to make sure you know something. You have rights. You can call me if anything like this happens again. The human resources team is here to help you."

"I didn't think I could complain," Monica said. "Kenny is my boss. He can call me whatever he wants, can't he?"

"No, Monica. He can't. Workers have rights too," Mrs. Wheeler said. "Don't ever forget that."

JUST *flip* THE BOOK!

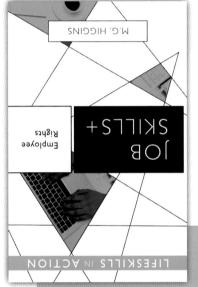

M.G. HIGGINS

Employee Rights

JOB SKILLS+

LIFESKILLS IN ACTION

US workers have rights. They must be treated fairly. Want to learn more about your rights as a worker?